T0369363

Hope This Helps

Poetry For the Coping Individual

R. B. Lane

HOPE THIS HELPS
POETRY FOR THE COPING INDIVIDUAL

iUniverse books may be ordered through booksellers or by contacting:

iUniverse
1663 Liberty Drive
Bloomington, IN 47403
www.iuniverse.com
844-349-9409

ISBN: 978-1-6632-6178-6 (sc)
ISBN: 978-1-6632-6177-9 (e)

Library of Congress Control Number: 2024906316

Print information available on the last page.

iUniverse rev. date: 03/27/2024

Life Is Terrifying Right Now

And like, maybe a little overwhelming, and I kind of have too much going on. Plus, there are tasks that require me to go out into public and, look, I'm just not ready to have another panic attack, okay? I am just absolutely ready to tear my hair out! Did you know people are not biologically made to handle such lengthy amounts of stress? No shit! And yet, here we are, overcomplicating our existence with all of these meaningless tasks and expectations. MOST OF WHICH, have absolutely no meaning or to true survival. I mean, like, if you were stranded and you had the choice between burning your pile of money to cook food you can eat or starving with a big pile of money, chances are you are going to pick the food, because money doesn't have any real value. Oh shit, I haven't gotten anything I was supposed to get done, DONE, because I've been sitting here stressing about it to you.

Why Cry Over Dandelions

As I finish the last steps of smoothing my pavement
I sit back, sigh, and I feel proud in my work,
To make something stronger than what was there before.
It settles and dries
And as I wait, I cry,
To think I might have something firm,
Something more.

Once it is hard
I take my first step
Onto the path I have paved for myself.
It is sturdy and,
Might I brag,
Smooth as I follow it in the directions I need to travel.

But suddenly ahead,
Right in the middle of my way,
A dandelion grown straight through the concrete!
Around in crumbles
My concrete tumbles
To the side
And away
So easily.
Then, as I look ahead
I'm filled with further dread.
I walk my path
And see even more clearly.
That the further I get

The more dandelions I've met,
My path becoming blurry.
And to my surprise,
Right before my eyes,
My trail dwindles into rubble and dandelions.

I cry through loss and through pain.
For now, I am incredibly drained
And my path overtaken by florets.
How something so small
Could stop me,
Through it all,
Tip my scales,
And leave me upset.
I will try another day,
Avoid being led astray,
For the solid path that I seek.
So, as I laid my head
And wished that I was dead
I felt the distance looked bleak.

Shhhhhhhhhhhh.... You don't see me.

Starving Artist

I paint myself to sleep.
I write lines for me to eat.
My substance is the art,
The very air in my lungs contrite.

"Keep moving," they say
And my hands do, for sure.
But, my mind is never clear;
The fog bittersweet.

A brush scratches the canvas,
Another stroke to life's madness;
The scrapes stuffing my soul with sounds bleak.

Put your nose to the grindstone
But my snout is already ground.
Why must existing be browbeat?

I just want to breathe
But the pollution fills my lungs
And the poison makes me dead meat.

My poems must be happy!
Not too depressing or dappy
But my legs shake and say,
"Take a seat."

There's a game for me to win,
Much to my chagrin;
And honestly,
I'd rather not compete.

I Feel like an Ant

"I feel like an ant,"
She said,
"So insignificant and small.
Barely even noticeable;
The most minuscule of all!"

Ants move the earth,
They take things in stride.
Their homes are tiny hills
With entire cities inside!

"What are you saying?"
She replied.

Though you feel infinitesimal
And others may agree,
Beneath the surface you're millesimal;
As far as the eye could see.
Though molehill, you seem,
Beneath you're a mountain.
Overflowing with potential,
A grand, exquisite fountain.

"I am weaker than I hope to be,"
She cradled her face in her hands.

Alright, let me put it this way,
So that you understand.
Ants may suffer under the beam,
Through the looking glass,
But as teeny weeny as they seem
Their strength cannot be passed.
The sun may scorch all manner of living,
Many fall prey and die by the blast.
But not all can put forth the toughness you're bringing;
Your might cannot be surpassed.

What they SAY isn't what you ARE.

Tripping on the Curb

I just want to walk down this sidewalk.
Keep my feet steady,
My stance firm.
But, I keep tripping on the curb.
Every street crossing,
Every time the path becomes bursting with bustling bargers,
I'm tripping on the curb.
I don't see anyone else trip,
All of them going about their days,
Faceplant-free.
Their legs don't wabble,
Their soles squeak soundly
And interweave an infallible rhythm
With the clickety-clack of equally auspicious heels.
But here I am,
Tripping on every curb.
I wish my feet worked so well,
Wish that I could be so smooth
But again I-
Don't trip?
I look down and see that I've stepped onto grass.

In stumbling grumbles,
Surrounding me are people tripping on the little divots
throughout
But my feet are unyielding
On the ground that suits my stride.
Memories of hard pavement and curbs fade
For I am on land meant for me.

I look back,
Just in time,
To see somebody trip on a curb.
I smile and I jog jubilantly to the juncture,
Reaching for their hand.
Because even if you trip on curbs,
There is always grass to soften your fall and find your footing.

R. B. LANE

Put. The. Coffee. Down.

Much has changed
And much has happened.
It's not the same
But not a bad thing.
Stress impressed upon your bones
Can leave you feeling quite alone.
So, take a break
And take a breather.
In
Then
Out
Or you'll get weaker.
You need some peace,
Some quiet time.
Take a nap
And you'll be fine.
Drink some water,
Eat some food
And you're in for a better mood.
Though your matters all are pressing,
YOU matter too
So, please,
Stop stressing.

Life Sucks.

It sucks because I suck. I mean, I haven't even showered in 5 DAYS. If I can't even take care of myself how in the HELL am I supposed to be trusted with anything else?! I'm just gonna stay here, in my bed, where everybody is safer from me and my inability. I can be a human burrito, a HAPPY human burrito. I can be happy, right? Super happy. The happiest! Sure...

I am not happy. Okay... I'll take this day and I will just rest up. I'll take a me day! Like, I know I just took a me week, and I NEED. TO. GET. UP. But I am stuck, and this bed is the only comfort I can feel...

Gravity

Gravity weighs heavily today
And it could, even tomorrow.
But, come what may,
There will be a day
When the weight dissolves away.
You will walk with strength;
From your path, you won't stray.
You will outshine the supernovas and suns that light
the day.
Overcast skies may join the fray
But you will face them,
With gravity to ground you,
And make them rue the day.

A handful of cheerios does not count as a meal... neither does a cup of coffee, an energy drink, that candy bar you grabbed at the gas station, a cake pop, the bag of chips you substituted for your lunch, the banana you ate on break, or the handful of gummy bears you grabbed on your way out of the house.

Bare Branches

Your leaves have fallen
You look as you feel
Dead to the world
Life doesn't seem real

The winter has come
Chills cut to your core
Your branches are bare
No green anymore

Your substance is gone
Just bones of what you were
No blooms to grace you
You barely stir

But spring will come
The sun return
While you freeze now
The frost will burn

Your buds will stretch
To bask and warm
Life will return
Your grace reform

R. B. LANE

The evergreens mock
They thrive in the cold
No mind to fallen leaves
Their needles keep hold

But a great oak you are
To change, you must
Autumn may come
And things seem a bust

Your branches are bare
But wait just a little
For the season's change
And your death's acquittal

Forget-Me-Not

The small flower swayed in the breeze,
Wondering why those passing called her beautiful.

Her stem dry,
Her leaves withering,
Petals wilting.
She could barely hold herself up
And yet…

They still called her lovely.
She couldn't be,
Could she?

Her roots, themselves, were destructive.
The concrete she had pushed through crumbled where
she grew.
Every inch she climbed towards the sun scorched her
And thus left her path demolished.

Why did she continue to climb?
She wondered.
The Sun smiled upon her,
Its heat blazing.

And so, she stood,
As passerby made their comments
And she continued to fade.
Forget-Me-Not.

R. B. LANE

White Walls

It took a day to even begin to write this,
Whether lack of wording or motivation,
I'm not sure.

Though what I will tell y'all,
Before my sanity stalls,
Is that I've been staring at the
Same.
Four.
White.
Walls.

These white walls?
They shield me,
Protect me.
But as attention goes,
They always neglect me.
They are all I have to see
Day in and day out.
A protective fortress
For my fears to run about.
But I will always cherish them,
Forever, you see.
For, I don't wish to trade them
For another set,
I plea.

Lunar Eclipse

Your soul is the moon
And it has many phases.
Though hope may be a sliver
There will always be changes.

Waxing and waning,
Sometimes without boon;
Our faith ebbs and flows,
And it will return soon.

Even when eclipsed,
Bathed in Earth's silhouette,
Your radiance stays!
So, don't you forget!

Unseen to you,
The tides follow command.
Much life, you supply
And every grain of sand.

Your moon may set
And disappear in the sun's flare.
But don't frown or fret,
The moon's always there.

Have you drank any water today?

Playing Hangman with Life

Letter to Hades

Hades,
Why do you call so strongly?
Why does each minute of every day pulse with the
promised whispers of time run out?
The hushed tones just unintelligible under the hoarse cries
of my pain.
I beseech thee, Hades!
Take me not to the underworld!
Let not the roots of blooms yet to come wither and fade;
Let not my suffering end here.
For, I see battles to come and people worth defending.
Allow my back to hold more weight,
My shield to deflect more blows,
My feet to carry on more tasks!
For my time is not finished until
I see more sunshine to bask in for my children's children,
More trees whose shade is shared with friends whose time
concludes past mine,
More tales read to sleepy faces
And eyes learning of new places!
No, my time is not finished yet.
My body is barren, why take my soul too?
Why cast your greedy hands upon this life?
One, which, I will not readily give and will fight for
As deeply as I have fought many a battle before.

With greatest respect,
The Unprepared Soul

The Flame That Lights My Cigarette

My shoes scrape on concrete,
Soaked through with icy puddle muck.
As I make my way about my day
The rain becomes a sheet of frozen torment.

I see others hesitate in entryways,
Opening umbrellas or pulling up hoods.
But I trudge forward begrudgingly,
Every drop of sharp pain a reminder that I am still here,
Still a part of this world.
But this world is full of gray,
Full of rain,
Full of icy puddle muck squelching between my toes.

I pause in my heavy steps,
Prepared to cater to my addiction,
When I realize,
The only thing brightening my face
Is the flame that lights my cigarette.

An object in motion wants to stay in motion and an object at rest wishes to stay at rest. It takes more energy to move when you stay stagnant for so long. Its not you, it IS HARD, but you WILL make it.

Scream

I once had seizures.

A weird way to start a poem
But, then again,
What about me doesn't perplex?

But I did.
I tried many medications,
My memories from that time still faded,
Like flowers you flatten into a book only to be left on the
top shelf,
Collecting dust,
Crumbling unseen.

One thing I do remember
Because I live through it every day.
Silently screaming,
Calling for help,
Frantically reaching out to those around you.
I lay a suicide note in your hand and you tell me how well
its written.
You comment on its punctuation and flow
And tell me that it could *definitely* publish.

I remember.
As I seized in the bed
All you saw were the physical convulsions,
The ones making you panic and seek help elsewhere.
You didn't see what I saw, did you?
My eyes were rolled back,
My mouth frothed as if I had forgotten my rabies shot.

But from where I was
The world was a dark void,
Only one spotlight.
No matter what I did, I couldn't escape it.
Even to take one step into the darkness to uncover why it
engulfed me.

Inside of my seizures,
I screamed until my voice was hoarse,
But all you heard were murmurs and mumbles.
That all you hear now, isn't it?
You can't hear me screaming.

Skip, Skip, Hush, Hush

Skip,
Skip,
Skipping on the mountainside.
Tip-
Toe,
Tipping through the woods.
A great, great many have since ventured here
But I'll be the one that stays for good.

Hoist,
Hoist,
Hoist me up to the trees!
Shush,
Shush,
Shush any words.
I want to swing, I want to fly!
Raise me up to the sky
To go a-sailing with the birds!

Hush,
Hush,
Hush, our little secret.
Quiet,
Quiet,
Quiet your hammering heart.
I promise I will see you at the new dawn
And you will see me unchanged from the start.

Hop-
Hip,
Hoppy up to my side!
Left,
Right,
Left and then you're there!
I'll be waiting for you always.
Until then, I feel that you still care.

Wipe,
Wipe,
Wipe away the tear drops.
Turn,
Turn,
Turn up that frown.
I'll be here until you find me,
And join me in my bed of ground.

Trauma, But Not
Blunt Force

The Apple

The apple will fall
From the tree whence it came.
But it will not remain,
Nor will it stay the same.

The apple will fall
And surely bruise its skin.
A dimple on the outside
But browned fruit within.

Discarded from the tree
But still kept close.
A prison of proximity
For the waste it loves the most.

The apple seeds will be its legacy,
All to remain of what we see.
For while it may fall near,
The apple doesn't rot far from the tree.

Glass woman

Glass woman walking down the street,
She doesn't mind how it scrapes her feet.
Every step they wear away.
Grain by grain her sand will stay
In her wake and on her way.
She will make it!
Day by day.
Glass woman's feet cease.
Her body gone,
Trail left to lay.
It slowly fades in the breeze.

A rope may tie, but it can also sever.

R. B. LANE

Losing It

I've been staring at the same spot in the ceiling.
Where it cracks
And it splits
Down into little bits…

Crumbles down.
Just like me,
instanity,
My heart pumping my blood in a blitz.

The window taps too,
Gray sky filled anew,
As I wait for eternity.
I continue my toil,
Keep burning my oil,
And wait for my mind to flee.

(Instanity- Instant insanity. Definitely only ever experienced by me, for sure. This poem is 1000% totally NOT describing my first experiences with depersonalization and derealization, which are completely normal trauma responses.)

Generational

Choking on a world
In which you have created.
We are lesser than
Or so you've demonstrated.

We dare to live our own lives,
Much to your chagrin.
And so you try to tear us down
Because you want to win.

Your ways are based so shallow,
Your need for imaginary stature.
You forget we are your daughters and sons,
Focus on wins you wish to capture.

While we wish for love,
You always wish to be right.
So quick to tear our peace asunder
For even the smallest slight.

So, for peace of mind,
body,
And soul
I'm stepping away,
I'm letting go,
And I will see you when the time is right.

You are NOT them. You are your own,
independent chronicle. Write your story, leave
theirs in your shadow. They may want to write
notes in your margin, but the narrative is all you.

R. B. LANE

Flashbacks

Panicked breaths echo in my head,
Wrists captured,
Mind filled with dread.
The blank sets in.
My toes,
Then feet.
Numb it away,
Let all thoughts fleet.
It is midnight
And I want to see
Not a peek.

I wasn't kidding...

Cosmic Burns Lit
by a Firestarter

You are like an ancient deity to me...
But, like, the one that plays cruel games with the humans in his care and needs to be usurped at all costs.
You are like a whole world to me...
But specifically, that planet where it rains glass... sideways.
You are like the sun to me...
If I get too close, I feel like I am going to die.
You are like Venus...
Way too close to the sun and when you're around, I'm pretty sure it's raining sulfuric acid.
You are the asteroid to my planet...
And by that, I mean stay the fuck away.
You are the Moon to my Earth,
And by that, I mean we need to keep a healthy distance and if you were to touch me it would be world ending.
You are the Pluto to my Sun...
Yeah, that would be the distance needed to be healthy.
You are like Haley's Comet...
Seeing you once in a lifetime is good enough.
Uranus...
Yep, that's where you need to shove it.
You are like Mercury...
People usually forget you and you are faster and smaller than they expected.

R. B. LANE

You are like Saturn...

Tons of rings but you can't get anybody to accept one because they come with the promise of debris flying at deadly speeds. Hard pass.

You are like Jupiter...

Pretty nice to see from afar but under the surface is a massive, catastrophic storm able to engulf and kill four earths and somehow managing to stay cold as fuck with all that friction.

Neptune...

Keep going! You still haven't reached that healthy distance yet!

You are the Earth...

And by that, I mean I'm pretty sure you are a lost cause and I would like to go find a planet more promising.

The Morality Paradox

Shed a tear for those in need,
Provide tax cuts for those with greed.
Say a prayer for those who hunger,
Waste all extra and never wonder.
Tell the masses they should be smarter,
Take away schools from the self-starter.
Hope for the children without homes,
Leave them on the streets, beaten and alone.
Tell the women "We are saving lives,"
And laugh with triumph as they die.
Here lies the morality paradox,
May it rest in pieces.

Story Time

Take a Brain Break

The Traveler of Many Swords

On a morning with glistening dew
A traveler found himself with few
A chance to live.
Surrounded by enemies,
He grabbed up a sword,
And with renewed power,
Those he slew.

His blade glistened with new life to him after the
onslaught
And with himself he fought,
To understand the view.
What was blood lust turned to love,
As the sharp edge shone with ominous glory before him,
The more blades,
The more power!
All the protection I need!
Still, thus,
I digress.

His collection immensely expanded,
Grew till he could not carry it bare-handed.
The traveler of many swords had to adapt;
He got himself a cart,
And the struggle was for naught.

The traveler of many swords,
So fine and so few,
Where will thy road have taken you?
Where will your tale,
Your prophecy end?
Where will your choice
Choose you to send?

From that day forth the man was obsessed,
He lusted for each new blade he possessed.

Carefully loaded his cargo,
And he began his journey as any man did.

The traveler of many swords,
So mean and so many,
Can you reach the Where with Any?
Where will your tale,
Your prophecy end?
Where will your choice
Choose you to send?

He moved quite swiftly on the start of his ride,
His cart moving as quickly as the tide,
And he hummed to himself as he approached a fork in
the road,

The horse was cut free by the barrage of blades
And trotted himself away
For somewhere to graze.
Wholeheartedly merry with his cruel, sharp load.
And as he called for the horses to slow their pace
Through the cart
And through the traveler's face
Every sharp, cruel blade did slide.
The traveler lay still.
For, from every direction
He was impaled
By his own protection.

The Game of Life

The game of life is like chutes and ladders
But if you're poor,
It's just chutes.

Unless you win the lotto.
Then,
It's a ladder to a mountain top view.

Some start the game with many ladders
And when they see those on the bottom,
They see a ladder for them to climb.
So, to them,
It's all the same.

But, from the base
Looking up
It's a one-way chute down
And at the top,
They tell them,
"It's a shame."

On the floor
It takes a ladder to get a ladder
But when they try to obtain,
Much to their distain,
It becomes a chute.
Still, from the sky,
It's the bottom they blame.

Many ladders, the top has,
And those they could share!
They say, "Build your own ladders!"
Still, it's not fair,
Cause the ground level has no wood for the frame.

The top fears chutes
And they secretly fear
That if one person came up
Chutes would appear.
So, they cling to their claim.

Modern Day Love Cliché

A new day has dawned!
The turn of the century has begun.
A new era has come on
And I relish to be player one!

My feet, they fly,
And so does the time
To enjoy just a moment with you.
To think that, perhaps, this hour may end
I cling to my cordless controller
And promise that you're player two.

I glow at the thought of your smile
And your laugh brings tears to my eyes.
I loathe the chance that you may depart.
And to see your stats, I cry.

We game anew each and every day.
It spears my soul that this time is fleeting;
That your grin will fall, or time expire.
So, I merk at every meeting.

So, join me for a moment
And feel the console's blessing.
We have no time to lose-
-Crap, there's an update.

I feel the power of this bond.
I know it cannot be vanquished
So, let's write a cliché, my love.
Together, we can play out our anguish.

My Heart Stays Where the Daffodils Would Grow

My heart stays
Where the daffodils would grow.
A thorned tree cage
Where nobody would go.
Where spring fledglings nest
And only we would know.
In a time that fades
So long ago.
When we were but kids
And wished for time to slow.
My heart stays
Where the daffodils would grow.

FIN

As if you ever finish coping…maybe a second volume?

Printed in the United States
by Baker & Taylor Publisher Services